A **customer** is the most
important person ever in this company …

A **customer** is not dependent on us,
we are dependent on him.

A **customer** is not an interruption
of our work, he is the purpose of it.

We are not doing a favor by serving him,
he is doing us a favor by giving us
the opportunity to do so.

~ Leon Leonwood ("L.L.") Bean ~

SERVE RIGHT

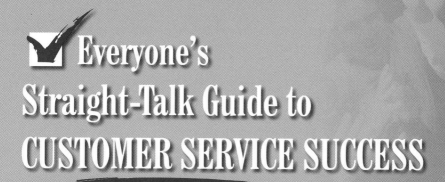 Everyone's
Straight-Talk Guide to
CUSTOMER SERVICE SUCCESS

STEVE VENTURA

WALKTHETALK.COM

Resources for Personal and Professional Success

To order additional copies of this handbook, or for information on
other WALK THE TALK® products and services,
contact us at
1.888.822.9255
or visit
www.walkthetalk.com

SERVE RIGHT

Printed in the United States of America
10 9 8 7 6 5 4 3 2 1

ISBN-13: 978-1-885228-90-1
ISBN-10: 1-885228-90-2

Edited by Marelen Burgett
Printed by MultiAd

51295

9 781885 228901

Contents

INTRODUCTION

We want it, we need it, we expect it, and we rely on it.

We talk to others about it. It's a regular part of our lives – something we experience almost every day, in one form or another. When we get it, sometimes it's great ... sometimes it's just okay ... and, all too frequently, it's not very good at all. *It* is:

CUSTOMER SERVICE.

And providing it is what your job is all about.

When you accepted employment with your organization, you took on a significant responsibility: taking care of the people who keep your business IN business. No job is any more important than that; no function is more closely linked to your organization's mission and its overall success.

Like it or not, you have some heavy weight on your shoulders. That's a fact! And along with that fact come a few logical and revealing questions to ponder:

How well do I meet that all-important responsibility?
How skilled am I when it comes to serving others?
How much do I really care about what I do at work?

Am I a true service professional – or just someone who's putting in time and collecting a paycheck?

So, how did you respond to those questions? How do you suppose your customers and coworkers would answer them ... about you?

Whether you're a seasoned employee with years of customer service experience or someone just starting in that field, no matter if this is your ideal job or just one stop on a larger career journey, you need to be successful. This book will show you how!

So, pay attention to what you're about to read. You owe that to *your organization* – the one that not only hired, trained, and pays you, but also has entrusted you with its resources, its mission, and its future. You owe it to *your customers* – the ones who depend on you and rightfully expect to receive the best service possible in exchange for their hard-earned money. Most importantly, you owe it to YOURSELF – the one who must live with the image you see in the mirror ... the one who ultimately benefits from, or is hurt by, the actions you take and the employment track record you add to each day.

On the pages that follow, you'll find **twenty-five "to do's"** – a collection of ideas, mindsets, and proven strategies guaranteed to help you deliver the high-quality service that your organization expects and that your customers deserve. They're written in a "pull no punches" style, so get ready for some straight talk. Get ready for the straight scoop.

USE and APPLY the information in this handbook, and you'll not only improve your overall effectiveness, but you'll also build a reputation (and a legacy) as a top-notch business professional who **thrives rather than merely survives** – someone who ...

SERVES RIGHT!

As you read this book you'll come across our **Solution Finder!** Visit WalkTheTalk.com where you can immediately access our free tips to help you achieve personal and professional success!

If you love
your customers to death,
you can't go wrong.

~ Graham Day ~

Serving RIGHT

Remember why your job exists.

Take a moment, right now, and do something that most people rarely (if ever) do: think about the purpose of your job. Here's the question to ponder: Why did your organization create your position ... why does your job exist?

Let me give you a couple of clues. The answer ISN'T so you'll have someplace to go several days each week. And it's NOT to enable you (with a paycheck) to buy stuff and do your part to "fuel" our economy. To be sure, those are positive byproducts – but they're not why your job is needed ... not why it was created.

Fact is, your job – *everyone's* job – exists for one primary purpose: to either make or do things for other people. Those "other people" – which include patrons of your business and coworkers in other departments – have a label: they're called CUSTOMERS. As such, *they* are the real source of your income ... *they* are the real reason you have been blessed with employment. And if *they* ever stop needing your services, so will your organization. NOT GOOD!

So, if you ever catch yourself thinking *I wish people would leave me alone for a while so I can get my work done*, here's what I recommend you do: Reach behind you, whack yourself on the back of the head, hope like heck that your wish is *never* granted, and then get back to doing what it is you're there for:

SERVING CUSTOMERS!

Put the customer first.

There was a day, not that long ago, when I hit the trifecta of poor customer service. I remember it far too well. It all happened when I went to a local restaurant for lunch. Driving through the lot, in an effort to avoid parking in the "boonies," I noticed one vacant spot right in front of the restaurant entrance. I sped up to take advantage of this good fortune, but alas, another car pulled into the slot as I was approaching. Although slightly ticked at first, I realized that "Hey, some other guy merely beat me to it." And I quickly became okay with what had occurred. Okay, that is, until the other guy exited his car and I saw that he was wearing a restaurant uniform. Now I was *really* ticked! I don't care if he wanted a good parking spot; so did I. And after all, I was the customer. I considered taking my business elsewhere, but I didn't. I parked way in the back and went in for lunch.

There was a line of people waiting for tables. I got in the back of it and slowly worked my way forward. Finally, I made it to the front of the line. Just as the girl behind the register desk was about to address me, two on-duty employees came up to her and asked for their paychecks. The girl looked at me, said, "I'll be with you shortly," and began a three-minute search for the employee checks – while I, the customer, was left waiting.

Finally, I got my table, made my order, ate my lunch, and was ready for my tab so I could pay up and leave. My waiter, however, was nowhere in sight. I sat semi-patiently for several minutes, and then got up and walked across the room – looking for someone to help me. I spotted another waiter and asked if he could get my bill. His response: "I'm sorry, I just started my break. I'm sure your waiter will be back shortly." With that, he walked away. Eventually, I got and paid my bill – and I walked away, too. And I haven't been back since.

One day, one place, three examples of employees putting their own needs and wants before those of a customer. Maybe they didn't think about what they were doing. Maybe they just didn't care. Either way, there will be one *less* patron contributing to their future income.

Here's the deal: When I choose to do business with a business, I don't expect its employees to act like I am royalty and they are medieval peasants. I do, however, expect them to make me feel special and important; I expect them to act like they understand (and appreciate) that I am the one who *really* pays their salaries ... that I am the reason their business exists. Show me that courtesy and you have a customer for life. Fail to do so, and I'm history.

As a customer, have you had experiences similar to the ones I described on the previous page? Did they make you as mad as they did me? If so, remember them ... learn from them ... make sure you don't do the same things to the people *you're* there to serve.

If you don't care, your customer never will.

~ Marlene Blaszczyk ~

FREE ... A Letter to Every Employee About the Importance of Customer Service
Go to *www.walkthetalk.com*

Respect their time.

I don't know about you, but I absolutely hate it when organizations that I choose to do business with – and give my hard-earned money to – act as if their time is important and mine is meaning-less.

Historically, doctors' offices have been notorious for this. You know how it goes. You're there for your 9:45 AM appointment. You check in with the receptionist, grab a chair and a magazine, and begin to wait – hoping that you'll actually be called in within the next several minutes. 10:00 AM comes and you're still reading. 10:10 ... 10:20 ... 10:30 – you're now on your third magazine and you still haven't heard squat. You go to the receptionist and she says, "The doctor should be with you shortly" (which is code for, "I don't have a clue when your turn will come."). 10:45 rolls around and again you go to the receptionist. You tell her that you've been waiting for an hour. Now she gets testy and informs you that the doctor is busy and you'll just have to keep waiting. It doesn't matter that you, too, are "busy." You're just expected to patiently and graciously sit there – wastefully burning one of your most precious resources: your time. Then, finally, the nurse comes out and says, "The doctor will see you now," and seems bewildered that you're not happy and grateful.

Happy? Grateful? Are you kidding me? You've just experienced yet another example of terrible customer service. No information, no options, no apology, no respect for your time ... NO RESPECT FOR YOU! Unfortunately, such examples are all too common – and they're not exclusive to the medical profession. They happen in every type of service business – every time a customer becomes victim to the "W word" (WAIT). And they are situations that you, as a service professional, must avoid creating for *your* customers.

Clearly, the avoidable wasting of a customer's time is disrespectful. And no one in their right mind is going to pay you money to disrespect them. At least they won't do it for long. Bottom line: If you don't value your customers, change your thinking – or find another line of work. If you DO value the people who ultimately pay your salary, RESPECT THEIR TIME by doing things like:

♦   Be prompt on your service calls. Be there as promised.

♦   Keep customers informed about unavoidable delays.

♦   Give customers the option of rescheduling if you can't meet an appointment time.

♦   Be honest when communicating wait times. Don't say "just a few minutes," if you know it will actually be a half hour.

♦   Never leave phone customers on "hold" for over a minute without getting back to them with a status report. If you can't meet their needs quickly, ask for a phone number and call them back.

♦   Remember that the people you serve don't like their time wasted any more than you do when YOU are the customer.

Never let them feel invisible.

Be honest. Admit it. At least once in your lifetime you've thought about what it would be like to be invisible. You probably fantasized about what you would do, where you would go, who you would observe (careful now), and what conversations you would listen in on as the proverbial "fly on the wall" – not to mention the admission fees to movies and concerts you'd avoid paying. But, to be sure, of all the things each of us would do if we knew we'd been unseen, one of them ISN'T going to a business with both a need and an expectation to be helped.

When we enter a store, a shop, a governmental agency, or any other type of business, we expect to be seen, acknowledged, and dealt with promptly. Yet, far too often, the employees of those organizations act as if we – the people they're there to serve – are invisible. We stand at the counter, but the person behind it doesn't look up right away; we search for an item, but the employee stocking shelves a few feet away never offers assistance. It's as if avoiding eye contact in some way makes it okay to continue doing whatever they're doing instead of helping us. Well, IT DOESN'T! It's NOT okay!

Fact is, failing to acknowledge and help customers – even if it's merely to say, "Thanks for coming in. I'll be with you shortly," – is rude, inconsiderate, and unprofessional. It's the epitome of bad service … a poor business practice. And anyone who does it, including you and me, is a poor business practitioner. Don't let that "shoe" fit YOU!

Most customers are reasonably patient people. They're typically willing to wait their turn – as long as you're serving someone else, acknowledge their presence, and get to them as fast as you can. But if you're not helping another customer, you better be helping THEM.

Customers don't care what your job is (or isn't). They don't care how busy you are or what your break schedule is. And most of them won't accept (shouldn't *have* to accept) being ignored – by *anyone* who works for your organization.

Act like the people who come to you for service are invisible, and they just might become that … they just might disappear. And then so might your job!

Although your
customers won't love you
if you give bad service,
YOUR COMPETITORS WILL!

~ Kate Zabriskie ~

Ask, don't tell.

Looking to ratchet up the quality of service you provide? If so, I've got five words for you:

THE CUSTOMER IS IN CHARGE!

Despite beliefs to the contrary held by some service UNprofessionals, you really work *for* each customer that does business with you. He or she has a need (or want), he or she has come to your organization to fill that need, and he or she is the one who will "foot the bill." Yep, the customer is in charge (or at least *should* be). You need to remember that. More importantly, you need to *behave* like you remember it. How do you do that? You do it by **asking rather than telling** ... by using phrases like:

May I put you on hold while I look into this?
instead of
I'll put you on hold and check.

Do you mind waiting while I find out for you?
instead of
Wait here, and I'll see what I can find out.

What would be a good time for me to get back with you?
instead of
I'll call you with an answer later this morning.

Somehow, someway, for some reason, a lot of businesspeople have lost sight of a very important principle: service is about doing things at the customer's convenience, not the server's. Don't be one of them. Ask instead of tell, and you'll not only demonstrate that the right person (the customer) is in charge, you'll also extend a common courtesy that lets your patrons know they are valued and appreciated. Make sense? (that was me *asking* ... instead of telling).

Never end with "can't."

If there's one thing I *can't* understand, *can't* condone, and *can't* accept, it's customer service people who tell me what they **can't** do for me ... and leave it at that. I mean, come on. Do they really think that's "service"? Do you?

Misguided fool that I may be, I believe that serving customers means doing things for people, helping them, addressing their issues, fixing their problems, and trying your absolute best to make them happy. That's what you're there to do ... that's what gets those people you rely on (for your livelihood) coming back. But you sure wouldn't know that by observing the inaction of a lot of service people in action. It's as if they think their corporate slogans are:

We're Here to NOT help!
If It Can Be Done, We CAN'T Do It!
Give Us the Chance to Say NO!
Tell Me How I CAN'T Help You!

Unfortunately, the scenario is all too familiar for many of us. You make a request; the person working with you cites a prohibitive policy. You suggest a remedy; you're told that's not how things work. You question a procedure; you hear, "I don't make the rules." You wonder why you even bothered to contact "Customer Service"; you have no good answer. You leave frustrated; your server leaves for a break. You tell others about the lousy service you received today; the employee tells others about the lousy customer he or she waited on today. Another great experience for the record books. NOT!

Believe me, I'm not a total idealist. I understand that customers can have far-too-lofty expectations and make unrealistic requests that just plain cannot be accommodated. And yes, you do have rules, procedures, and guidelines that you have to follow as you serve the patrons of your organization. Sometimes, you really can't do what people want you to do. But consider this: for every "can't" there usually is a "can" – something else you can do ... some alternative that you can offer and deliver on.
And doing that is what good service is all about.

So, never end a business interaction with a negative ... with an explanation of your inability to act. The next time you find yourself needing to tell a customer, "I can't do that," tack on this short, powerful, and service-oriented phrase:

"But here's what I *can* do ...."

Those are the exact words I heard from an airline employee after a fairly recent trip I made to attend a family reunion in California. I had arrived precisely on time at my chosen destination ... my luggage, however, had gone somewhere else. It was misplaced. After several hours of waiting, the bags eventually showed up. As I was collecting my late arriving suitcases – and after accepting the employee's sincere apology – I informed her that I felt the flight should be free ... that she should refund my entire ticket. (I really didn't expect that, but I figured it was worth a try.) She told me that she was not able to do that, but that she *could* give me a flight voucher for $100 and a handful of "beverage tickets" for my return flight. That's precisely what she did. And, I actually left happy ... almost glad my bags had been misplaced. Even though it wasn't what I had asked for, that woman found a way to DO something for me. I had been "served." As a result, I've given that airline several more opportunities to serve me since.

Keep your commitments.

Dependable. Reliable. Professional. Trustworthy. Do those words describe you? If asked, would your customers say that your word is "good as gold"? Could they cite specific examples of you coming through for them? Would they be *unable* to list times when you "dropped the ball" and forgot to follow up with them? The answer to each of those questions needs to be a resounding "yes," if you are going to do well in the service arena and build the successful career you want and need.

All top-notch customer service employees place a premium on keeping their promises and commitments. If they say they'll do something – whether "important" or seemingly insignificant (to them) – they remember it ... and they DO it. They count on the fact that customers can count on them. And they understand that statements like ...

I was gonna ... I meant to ...
I haven't forgotten ... I'll get to it soon ...
Something came up ... There's still time ...
I've been busy ...

all translate the same way: **I JUST DIDN'T DO IT!** Those are rationalizations. They're excuses. And from the customer's perspective, those words are pretty much meaningless. All the customer knows (and probably cares about) is that he or she was expecting something and was disappointed.

Has that ever happened to you? If so, you know how frustrating it can be.

With the exception of a few unethical jackasses out there, people really do *intend* to keep their word and honor their promises. But good intentions alone won't take you very far. You get no "points" for them.

Points come only when you deliver.

So, don't make promises lightly; don't make ones you can't (or really don't intend) to keep. And when you do make commitments to your customers:

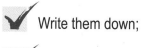 Write them down;

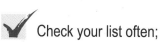 Check your list often;

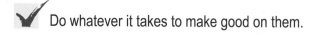 Do whatever it takes to make good on them.

Those people are expecting you to deliver on your commitments. Follow through.

Your reputation is at stake … your success is on the line.

> *Promises are like crying babies in a theater, they should be carried out at once.*
>
> ~ Norman Vincent Peale ~

Biggest question:
Isn't it really 'customer helping'
rather than customer service?

And wouldn't you deliver
better service
if you thought of it that way?

~ Jeffrey Gitomer ~

Learn from the best ...
and the worst.

It's a safe bet that you were exposed to some very powerful lessons on customer service prior to turning the first page in this book. In fact, you started receiving them well before you accepted employment with your organization. Where did they come from? Well, they came courtesy of all the business employees you've encountered since the time you first became a customer – with the more recent encounters probably being the most memorable.

Think back on the various people who have "waited on" you in the last year or two – employees who stand out in your mind. Some you may remember in a positive vein – some not so positively. It's likely that some bent over backwards to make sure you were satisfied and taken care of. These were terrific customer service pros who showed, by their example, what *you* should be doing now. Emulate them; follow their lead. When in doubt, ask yourself, "What would he do ... how would she handle this situation?" Then, DO IT!

Maybe your inventory of past service experiences also includes one or two jerks ... or people who just exhibited "jerkish" behaviors. Okay, you're right, they WERE jerks! They didn't seem to give a flip about making sure that your needs were met. And you'd probably just as soon forget them. DON'T! You need to remember them clearly and frequently. They provide your best lessons on what NOT to do! By avoiding the kinds of behaviors they exhibited, you'll make sure that, down the road, you don't appear on someone *else's* list of poor service experiences.

Cherish complaints.

There's an appropriate two-word response you should offer whenever a customer complains about your product or service – and it isn't an expletive. Know what it is? It's THANK YOU. And no, I haven't lost the grip with this one!

Here's a one-question quiz: Two customers enter your establishment and come to you. One hands you a T-shirt from his new clothing business while the other lodges a complaint about poor service she received. Which one has given you a gift? The correct answer is BOTH. And actually, the person with the complaint (you know, the one you thought was a pain in the butt) did you the *bigger* favor. If you think about it, she may have given you the two most valuable gifts you received that day:

1. Feedback you can use to improve the service (or products) you provide to her and others, and ...

2. The opportunity to address her concern, fix her problem, and – most importantly – keep her as a customer.

Believe me, I *do* understand how distasteful it can be to hear bad news. If you've had a long, tough day, the last thing you probably want to hear is somebody "whining" about their problem. Hey, you've got your own issues to deal with, right? Sure. But do you really want customers to keep their problems with your business to themselves? Do you really *not* want to know when you're missing the mark in the customers' eyes? Do you really want them to say nothing and merely take their business (and their money) elsewhere? Your answers to those questions need to be "no, no, and NO" – unless you really don't care about your job and your long-term career.

Let's be clear here, I'm not suggesting that complaints are "merit badges." They're not things you should seek; you don't need to try to earn as many as you can. That would be stupid (not to mention career limiting). Your goal should be to never give people reasons to complain at all. But, we're all human … we make mistakes … we don't always give the best service possible. And we all need to know when we have failed to satisfy the people who keep us in business.

So, the next time a customer complains about something you or someone else in your organization did or didn't do, remember that they are giving you a gift. It may be a gift in disguise, but it is one nonetheless.

Cherish it.
Learn from it.
Be grateful that you got it.

When it comes to customer **dis**satisfaction, ignorance is NOT bliss!

> Those who enter to buy, support me.
> Those who come to flatter, please me.
> Those who complain teach me how I may
> please others so that more will come.
> Only those hurt me who are displeased
> but do not complain.
> They refuse me permission to correct my errors,
> so that I may improve my service.
>
> ~ Marshall Field ~

Interesting tidbits ...

On average ...

Satisfied customers tell **5** people about good service they receive.
Dissatisfied customers tell **10** people about bad service received.

Hal Mather, The Performance Advantage

For every unsatisfied customer who complains, there are **26** other unhappy customers who say nothing. And of those 26, **24** won't come back.

U.S. Office of Consumer Affairs

The average company loses approximately **20%** of its customers each year.

Patricia Sellers, "What Customers Really Want,"
Fortune Magazine

Of customers who take their business somewhere else:
    15% find *cheaper* products elsewhere;
    15% find *better* products elsewhere;
    65% leave because of poor customer service.

The Forum Corporation

From: *180 Ways to Walk the Customer Service Talk*

Don't take their frustration personally.

Sooner or later it's bound to happen. Maybe it already has. A customer has an issue, gets totally frustrated, and he or she vents ("dumps") on the nearest representative of your organization – YOU!

Out of the mouth of this normally calm and nice person you hear verbal blasts such as: *This is ridiculous! ... What's wrong with you people! ... Is anybody around here competent! ... This place sucks!* It may be that you are the individual they have a problem with. Perhaps you're not. Either way, they're upset ... and they've taken you to a place many of us know far too well: TEMPTATION CITY.

So, what do you do? What *should* you do? Is your first reaction to view their accusations as "fightin' words" ... to want to blast back ... to think, "I'll see your rotten attitude and raise you an insult"? As tempting as those might be, you need to fight the urges. Reactions like that do nothing but put you smack dab in the middle of an ego contest in which no one is in control, no one is the voice of reason, and no one is getting or giving good customer service. In the end, the "contest" will conclude with no real winner, two losers, and you nominated as corporate poster child for self-inflicted career sabotage.

Here's the deal: In the heat of anger and frustration, people have a tendency to spout off without thinking ... to generalize ... to use words they really don't mean. When customers are frustrated, they often say things like, *You screwed up my order, again!* Most of the time, they're using "you" to mean your organization. Occasionally, they mean you the individual – the specific representative of your business. But probably in neither case do they mean you, the person. How could they? They don't know you. They don't know about your character, your beliefs, your values. And since they don't know you personally, they can't possibly be *attacking* you personally. So, there's really no need for you to defend yourself. Keep that in mind, and it's more likely that you'll keep a cool head and demonstrate the professionalism that your organization expects from you.

Does all this mean that you have to willingly accept verbal abuse? Of course not! But you don't have license to escalate the hostility either. If a customer crosses the line, you should immediately seek assistance from management or a coworker. Fortunately, that rarely happens. For most situations, you should have a simple goal in mind: to cut the person the same slack that you would want if you were in his or her shoes.

Borrowing a line from *The Godfather III* …

It's not personal. It's business.

Techniques for Dealing with Angry Customers

As long as they're not abusive, let customers with problems vent. Don't interrupt. Telling you their complete story, and describing how frustrated they are, allows customers to release pent-up negative energy. The sooner they let it out, the sooner they'll calm down.

One of the fastest and most effective ways to diffuse customer anger is to agree with them. Saying, "You've got a right to be mad," or "I can understand why you're upset – I would be, too," can literally stop an upset customer in their tracks. Their case has been made ... the fight they expected never happened. And, if the next thing you say is, "Let's see what I can do to make it right," you'll immediately take the discussion from negative complaining to constructive problem solving.

Ask customers to identify the solution they would like. Just be careful you don't say things like, "So, what do you want me to do about it?" Use a more tactful approach, like: "We want you completely satisfied. What would you consider to be a fair solution?" If you can meet their request, do it! If you can't, at least make sure you tell them what it is you CAN do.

Use "I" in place of "YOU"! One way to minimize tension is to keep your verbal finger pointed at you rather than the customer. See if you can feel the difference between these statement combinations:

What do you need? – What can *I* do to meet your needs?
You didn't complete the form. – *I* need a little more information.
You need to call this number. – Let *me* make a call for you.

Don't just *inform*, *PERFORM*.

So much of the "service" we get these days merely involves telling us stuff: *Your item is on backorder. Not sure when it will come in ... The installer should be there sometime tomorrow ... You'll need to call this number for help ... Sorry, we don't carry that part.* Wow! Geez! Thanks! Excuse me if I'm not overwhelmed! It's as if some employee name tags read Customer *Information* Representative instead of Customer SERVICE Representative. And I don't know about you, but I'm more interested in being truly served rather than just told.

To be sure, providing information is an important part of your job. But, as portrayed in the examples above, sometimes customers may conclude their dealings with you not knowing any more than they did the moment you said hello. If that's the case, it pretty much means that you really didn't bust your tail to *help* them. That ain't cool ... it's *not* okay. You need to *per*form as well as *in*form.

So, the next time you need to pass information along to a customer, ask yourself: What more can I do to help this person besides just informing? If you do, some of the examples above will sound more like this:

Your item is on backorder. There's no specific delivery time listed. Would you like me to find out when you can expect it?

There's a number to call for help. Would you like me to call it for you and talk with the representative myself?

Sorry, we don't carry that part. I'll be happy to call around and see if I can find someplace that does have it.

Make them *feel* right.

It's an age-old question stemming from a timeless business platitude: **Is the customer always right?** And now comes the best answer I can give you: IT DOESN'T MATTER!

Of course, we all know that people aren't perfect. So, no one can really be correct one-hundred percent of the time. But here's something you need to think about and remember: wondering whether or not customers are "always right" (or arguing that they *aren't*) is a waste of time. Why? Because it's totally irrelevant! Fact is, even if customers aren't always right, they ARE always customers. They are why your organization exists; they are the ones in control; they are the keys to your livelihood; they deserve the very best you have to offer. So even if they're wrong, it's your job to make them *feel* like they're right – if, that is, you want to get and keep their business.

Not long ago, I went to yet another restaurant with some friends. Admittedly, I made a mistake when placing my order with the waiter – although I didn't realize it at the time. When the food arrived, I said, "This isn't what I wanted." Rather than correct the problem and get me the item I thought I had ordered, the waiter chose to stand there and convince me that I was in error … that this was precisely what I had requested. I could have made a scene, but I didn't. I went ahead and begrudgingly ate the meal he brought me. As a result, I was unhappy (not to mention embarrassed), the waiter got no tip, and I haven't been back there since. He won the battle but lost the war.

Looking back on that evening, I know I wasn't right. But I was that waiter's customer. Next time I go out to eat, I'll be someone else's customer.

Remember your *internal* customers.

Several weeks before starting this project, I was talking to a friend of mine. He asked what I was working on. I told him I was about to begin writing a book on customer service. His response: "That's nice. Too bad it's not a book that applies to me – otherwise I'd want to get a copy." I asked why he thought customer service wasn't relevant for him. His answer revealed just how misinformed he was: "Because I don't deal with customers. I keep our computers running ... I've got an 'inside' job."

Sound familiar? Do you know someone like that? Do *you* have "a friend" who thinks that customer service applies only to front-line employees dealing directly with patrons who walk in your door or call on the phone? If so, your "friend" is as equally misinformed as mine. And both of them need to get their heads straight!

Fact is, everyone with a job provides some kind of service to other people. It doesn't matter if you stock shelves, run a website, manufacture parts, issue paychecks, or clean toilets – you're doing it for someone else.

That someone may be your boss, a fellow team member, or perhaps, a person in another department or location in your organization. And since they are the individuals you do things for, they share the same label with everyone from the *outside* who does business with you. They are

"CUSTOMERS."

They are *your* customers ... your *internal* customers. And as such, they deserve the very same courtesies, attention, effort, and quality work that "external customers" should receive. Why wouldn't they?

So, tell "your friend" to remember this: When it comes to the world of the employed, one way or another ...

everyone is in the customer service business!

Organizations have more to fear from lack of quality internal customer service than from any level of external customer service.

~ Ron Tillotson

Never "badmouth" the business.

Imagine this scenario: You go to a hardware store (or a yarn store, an auto parts place, or whatever) looking for an item needed to complete a project. You quickly discover that the business doesn't have what you're looking for. The person waiting on you has had a bad day but knows better than to mistreat you, so he or she directs their frustration at the organization: "Yeah, this place never has what people need. I don't know why they bother to come in. I wouldn't shop here!"

Seem far-fetched? It's not; it happened! It was a yarn shop. I was there with my wife. I have no idea what was bothering the employee who uttered that statement. Maybe she was upset with a coworker or her boss. Perhaps this was her way to even the score for some wrong she perceived came her way from upper management. It might even be that she wanted to make sure we knew that she was not responsible – and should not be blamed – for the store not having what we needed. Who knows?

Quite frankly I DON'T CARE what motivated her action, and I doubt that you would, either. It was bad form – and my immediate thought was: *If she worked for me, I'd fire her for that!* I must admit, however, that her attempt to ding the business was quite successful. Why? Because we took our business elsewhere. And, as with many of the other personal examples cited in this book, we can't imagine ever going back there again. But here's the kicker: That store lost our future business not because they didn't have what we wanted, but rather because they allowed someone with a bad attitude, like her, to deal with (and supposedly serve) deserving customers like us.

Hopefully, the "moral" of this true story is obvious: No matter the nature of your business, your goal should be to create a positive experience for each customer you serve. And you certainly *don't* do that by ragging on the very same organization that has given you employment – and whose paycheck you accept every week or two. From the customer's perspective, you ARE the business. Criticize it, and you're criticizing yourself … do things to drive customers away, and you're shooting yourself in the foot (not to mention sabotaging your career).

Got a work-related gripe, problem, or concern? Address it internally with the people who can do something about it. Feel frustrated occasionally? Get a stress ball and squeeze the snot out of it! But never, ever bad-mouth the business in front of a customer. You'll be much better off using your energy to make things better rather than whining about why they're not.

Compensate their inconvenience.

Here's a basic rule from *Customer Service 101*: **People should not be inconvenienced when they do business with you.** Wow, what a revelation! Seems like common sense, right? Maybe so. Yet most of us can cite examples of times when we have experienced just the opposite – when we had an unreasonable wait, when what we got was not what we ordered (or not working properly), or a myriad of other possibilities. Perhaps some of *your* clients can offer similar examples. And clearly none of those experiences would fall in the category of "strategies for making customers happy and getting their repeat business." Again, no revelation!

In the real world, occasional customer inconvenience is inevitable. We're human ... we make mistakes ... things don't always turn out right. STUFF HAPPENS. And when it does – when it happens with your customers – you need to sincerely apologize. But you don't stop there. You also need to make things right. And doing that involves not only correcting any errors that were made, but also compensating the customer for his or her inconvenience by providing something extra – a discount, an additional service, or a "freebie" item of some kind.

Doing that sends a message to the customer: *You should not have been inconvenienced, and we are going to make it up to you.* And it increases the likelihood that, instead of being upset, he or she will leave satisfied ... saying "thank you" on the way out.

Not sure what types of customer service "solutions" are available for you to offer? Check with your manager.

Customers don't expect you to be perfect. They do expect you to fix things when they go wrong.

~ Donald Porter ~

Watch your body language.

Here's a one-question, multiple choice quiz for you:

Which of the following communicates a message to customers?
> a. Rolling your eyes
> b. Tapping your fingers
> c. Frowning/scowling/sighing
> d. Shaking your head sideways
> e. All of the above.

Not exactly a tough one! Obviously the answer is "e" (All of the above). Each of those physical gestures – known as "body language" – sends a negative message ... without you saying a single word. Even if you combine them with positive verbiage, the communication is still negative.

Put yourself in a customer's shoes for a minute. The employee you're dealing with says, "How can I help you?" while frowning and tapping his fingers. What's he really saying? If you guessed something like *Actually, I'm not that interested in waiting on you*, you're two-for-two on this page – and you have a pretty good grasp of the power (and importance) of nonverbal communication.

There's an old adage that goes like this: It's not what you say but how you say it! Well, when it comes to customer service, that adage needs a little modification. Here's a different version to remember and apply:

It's what you say AND how you say it that counts!

To interact with customers effectively, ya gotta use the right words – and you have to accompany those words with gestures and tone that demonstrate sincerity … that SHOW you really mean what you're saying. And to do that, you have to monitor yourself; you have to constantly focus on what you're doing and how your customers are reacting to you.

Take a few minutes to make a list of the body language that you would consider insincere, disturbing, or inappropriate from someone who was serving you. Study that list, remember it, and do your very best to AVOID those behaviors yourself. Ask your colleagues for feedback on how you come across. And make a conscious effort to begin all customer interactions with eye contact and a smile. Those are two of the very best "messages" you'll ever send.

Research has shown that approximately **55%** of
all face-to-face communication is done through
BODY LANGUAGE
(facial expressions, posture, gestures)

Know your products and services.

Do you have a good working knowledge of all the various products or services your business offers? Do you take the time to study manuals, brochures, and industry publications? Do you use the items yourself? Can you accurately describe components, features, and warranties? Can you correctly answer common, typical questions about your offerings (or at least know where to find those answers)? Could you pass a test of basic information? If "yes," congratulations! You're on top of your job ... and you're prepared to serve the customers who come to you, call you, or write to you for assistance. If "no," WHY NOT? How in the world can you help others when you know as little as they do? The simple answer is, YOU CAN'T!

Your organization has a pretty reasonable expectation: that you know what you're doing – and that you'll become even more knowledgeable as time passes. Certainly, the business has an obligation to provide you with the training and information necessary to do your job. But your development is a *shared* responsibility. You own a large chunk of it as well. And that leads to the big question:

What specifically are you doing to meet that responsibility?

If you're falling short on answers to that one, it's time to get to work.

Do something extra.

Looking to build a great reputation, enhance your career, and turn satisfied customers into delighted ones? Then get into the habit of giving people more than they expect. As that familiar saying goes, you have to *under* promise and OVER DELIVER.

After you meet a customer's needs, look for one more thing – something extra – to do for them or give to them. It doesn't have to be big or costly. It can be as simple as helping them fill out a rebate slip. Perhaps it's giving them your name and phone number with instructions to call you if they have any problems. Or maybe it's just carrying an item out to their car. Whatever it is, that little extra can make a big difference in keeping customers happy ... and motivating them to come back again and again. Besides, you never know when a grateful patron just might contact your boss to say how terrific you are.

Clearly, many people in the service business haven't figured this one out yet. I've experienced more than a handful of supposed "service professionals" whose mantra seems to be *Only what is required and nothing more.* But that's okay, because the more folks like that who are around, the easier it is for you, me, and others to stand out and shine.

Here is a simple but powerful rule: Always give people more than what they expect to get.

~ Nelson Boswell ~

Help *others* serve.

Next to ensuring that its business practices are legal and ethical, nothing is more important for an organization than serving customers. **NOTHING!** That's why customer service is *everyone's* responsibility – regardless of whether you deal directly with patrons or work "behind-the-scenes" supporting customer contact employees. Everyone must pitch in ... everyone must contribute. As Jan Carlzon, former CEO of Scandinavian Airlines, so aptly said:

> *If you are not serving your customer,*
> *you better be serving someone who is!*

If I were in the business of writing job descriptions for organizations, that quote would appear in the "duties and responsibilities" section of every single one I wrote. You'd find it on job spec sheets for ...

... employees who stock shelves so that service reps can help customers find what they need;

... techno-wizards who keep websites and phone systems operating so that customers can get information, order products, and call-in for assistance;

... janitorial crew members who keep facilities clean for customers and employees alike;

... admin folks who staff, schedule, and pay the people who *serve* the people who pay the organization.

And to be sure, you'd find it (in BIG print) on job descriptions for those, like you, who work directly with customers.

Okay, let's cut to the chase. What does (or at least what *should*) all this mean for you? Well, if you're going to be successful in your job and meet your organization's expectations, you certainly need to provide the absolute best service possible to the customers you interact with. But it doesn't stop there. You also need to **help your coworkers** do that exact same thing. You need to support their efforts ... you need to teach them what you have learned ... you need to pitch in whenever you're free and they have customers waiting ... you need to look for opportunities to provide service rather than waiting for them to find you.

You see, customer service is a team activity. Everyone has the same overall purpose ... everyone should have the same goal. There's no such thing as "my customers" or "your customers" – there's only ...

OUR CUSTOMERS!

Those who get that will do just fine in business. Those who don't, won't.

FREE ... What Kind of Team Player Am I?
Go to *www.walkthetalk.com*

Watch your assumptions.

It's no secret that, as human beings, we're all prone to making assumptions. We often make them as we view the world around us. We make them about the people we have relationships with – even those we care deeply for. And yes, we make them in the course of our daily jobs. As a customer service professional, that's something you need to be conscious of – something you need to control.

Certainly, not all assumptions are bad. Some are wise and prudent to make. For example, it's safe to assume that you can always improve the quality of service you provide to others ... or that there's always more you can learn about your organization's products and services ... or that you can always do more to assist and support the people you work with. Those are productive thoughts that keep you on your toes and keep you focused on continual self-improvement. If you already make those kind of assumptions, keep doing it. If you don't, START!

But just as there are some assumptions that are okay to make, there's also a ton of unproductive ones you should avoid like the plague. And when it comes to serving customers, five top the list:

1. **Assuming you know what customers want – or what's best for them.**
   Unless you're clairvoyant or blessed with infinite wisdom (yeah, right), you need to spend less time telling and more time listening.

2. **Assuming customers know what they really need.**
   Sometimes they do, sometimes they don't. Your job is to help uncover their needs so you can appropriately fill them. Ya gotta talk, ya gotta probe. And once again, ya gotta LISTEN.

3. **Assuming customers understand everything you have explained.**
Information has little value if it isn't received and understood by those it's intended for. Develop the habit of always asking customers what you can explain further or clarify.

4. **Assuming customers are okay with whatever you do in the course of serving them.**
(see page 19)

5. **Assuming customers are happy and satisfied.**
You'll never really know unless they tell you ... or unless you check. So, if they don't say anything, ASK! *(My goal is to make sure you're happy and satisfied with the service you received. How did I do?)*

Think for a moment. What additional assumptions are counterproductive to good customer service? What others have you experienced yourself as a customer? Write them down in the box below. Periodically review them. Remember them. Most importantly: AVOID them!

You are serving
a customer,
not a life sentence.
Learn how to
enjoy your work.

~ Laurie McIntosh ~

Get *into* it ... or *out* of it.

Pretend for a moment that you have a good friend who works in customer service – but she isn't all that good at it. You offer her this book; she declines. She tells you that she's unhappy at work, that she doesn't really enjoy dealing with or helping customers, and that she has no interest in killing herself to give the best possible service. Then, she asks for your advice. What would you tell her?

There's a decent chance you'd say the same thing I would: "Ask for a transfer ... dust off your resume ... start checking the want ads. If you can't get into your job, you need to think about finding another line of work." That's the best advice I could give her. And it's the best advice I could give you ... should you ever find yourself in that fictional friend's shoes.

Fact is, customer service isn't right for everyone, and everyone isn't right for customer service. You have to like it. Helping people has to be important to you ... it has to be in your blood. Excuse the old cliché, but it is a "labor of love." And if you ever get to the point where it's *all labor* and *no love*, it's time to either ratchet up your caring or move on. To do otherwise would be a disservice to your customers, to your organization, and to YOURSELF.

Am I suggesting that every service employee who gets in a funk should quit? Of course not! That would be irresponsible (not to mention idiotic!) I'm merely saying that each of us has a job we were *meant* to do ... a job we can excel at and enjoy. If yours is serving customers, GREAT. If it's not, it's something else ... and it's waiting for you somewhere out there.

Tough talk? Perhaps. Straight talk? Definitely. Accurate talk? I believe so.

Don't let *your* work add to your *customer's.*

Here's another of those tough, one-question quizzes: Who would you say provides better customer service – someone who creates more work for you or one who creates less? Duh! Of course, it's the latter ... the person who eases your burden rather than adding to it. That's just more of that thing called "common sense." But common sense apparently isn't all that common – at least it's not for someone who "served" me a while back. It happened like this ...

I had just ordered our winter supply of firewood. The guy arrived to deliver it right on time. He stacked the wood neatly in the spot I had identified. Because he was so nice, friendly, and prompt, I gave him the payment check before he was finished stacking. He completed his work and left. Twenty minutes later I went out to check on and admire our future source of winter warmth. The wood was there alright – just as I had ordered. But something else was there as well: a mess. There were wood chips and sawdust and pieces of bark all over my driveway and backyard. It took me about an hour to clean it all up and get it looking like it did before he arrived. Needless to say, I wasn't happy. I paid good money for someone to do something FOR me, and I wound up getting something done TO me. I got the wood. I also got "the shaft!"

Sound familiar? Maybe you've never ordered firewood, but it's likely you have experienced situations in which someone else's work spilled over onto you ... times when you ended up having to do what others could have done, or should have done, for you. You know how frustrating it can be. Getting more than you bargained for isn't always a positive thing!

If you go to customers' homes to repair things, do you typically clean up after yourself – leaving the place the way you found it? *If so, that's good service. If not, it's NOT!*

If you provide information to customers over the phone, do you typically research things for them rather than merely giving them a bunch of other numbers to call? *If so, that's good service. If not, it's NOT!*

If you sell items that have rebates or warranties, do you help customers fill out the forms rather than just handing them a bunch of paperwork to complete on their own? *If so, that's good service. If not, it's NOT!*

If you manage financial portfolios, do you give your customers regular status reports rather than expecting them to locate and contact you? *If so, that's good service. If not, it's NOT!*

Whatever type of work that you perform, do you make a special effort to do things for customers rather than create additional work for them?

If yes, YOU PROVIDE GREAT CUSTOMER SERVICE.
If no, it's time for a change!

Develop an "attitude of gratitude."

One of the many observations I've made (and lessons I've learned) over the years is that successful people tend to be grateful people. They have attitudes ... the good kind of attitudes: **attitudes of gratitude**. With few exceptions, they're positive people who focus on the many things they *have* rather than the smaller number of things they *don't* have. They understand that, no matter how difficult a day or situation may seem, there's a ton of people out there in the world who would trade places with them in a minute. As a result, they look for, *and show*, appreciation for the positives (people, opportunities, circumstances, etc.) that are all around them – especially at work. These are the people who are absolute joys to be around and work with ... the ones we hope will be waiting on *us* when we choose to do business with their organizations. And if you're not already a member of their special group, you would be wise to join it as quickly as possible.

So, what should you be grateful for ... and how might you show it? Only you can truly answer that completely. But there are a few "universals" ... things to appreciate that are common to all business people – especially those in customer service. Here are two of them:

1. Appreciate the fact that you have a job. Not everyone today can make that claim, and that makes you one of the lucky ones. Whether or not you're in your dream position doesn't really matter in today's economy. You have work. You get a paycheck. Be thankful for that ... and *show* it by doing the best that you can – and by letting others know that you're happy to be a member of the team.

2. Appreciate the fact that you have customers to serve. Be happy that they choose to do business with you. Be proud that your organization trusts you enough to let you represent it – and to work with its most precious assets. Be thankful when customers come back to give you more of their money, again and again. And *show* your appreciation by giving those customers the best service possible – and by sincerely thanking them for allowing YOU to meet their needs.

Attitudes of gratitude are contagious. If you haven't done so already, get "infected." Then spread that virtuous virus around your workplace!

> **Keep a grateful journal.**
> **Every night, list five things you are grateful for.**
> **What it will begin to do is change your perspective**
> **of your day ... and your life.**
>
> ~ Oprah Winfrey ~

FREE ... Success-Killing Phrases
(and Thoughts) to Avoid
Go to *www.walkthetalk.com*

Talking Your Way to
SERVING RIGHT

The **10** important words to say:
"I apologize for our mistake. Let me make it right."

The **9** important words to say:
"Thank you for your business. Please come back again."

The **8** important words to say:
"I'm not sure, but I will find out."

The **7** important words to say:
"What else can I do for you?"

The **6** important words to say:
"What is most convenient for you?"

The **5** important words to say:
"How may I serve you?"

The **4** important words to say:
"How did we do?"

The **3** important words to say:
"Glad you're here!"

The **2** important words to say:
"Thank you."

The **1** important word to say:
"Yes."

Make "The Golden Rule" your #1 guideline.

It's an "old saying" – uttered seemingly forever – that is as familiar to us as the air that we breathe. It's a fundamental moral principle found in virtually all cultures around the world. Everywhere you look, now and throughout history, you find people espousing it as the key behavioral tenet. It never gets old or outdated ... it has never outlived its relevance or usefulness. It is **THE GOLDEN RULE** – perhaps, the most simple, profound, and universal guide for providing top-notch customer service.

Looking for a "crash course" on serving right? Here it is ...

Treat customers the way you would like to be treated.

Do unto customers that which you would have servers do unto you ... and the people you care about.

To the vast majority of people reading this who believe in, and live by, the Golden Rule, you have my admiration ... and I hope that one of you will be the next person serving me.

To the small minority who may think all this is lame and hokey, I wish for you service from people who think just like you!

Nothing else needs to be said.

WALK THE TALK.

No book on customer service could be complete without addressing the most basic (and most important) employee responsibility of all: Serving With Integrity. You meet that responsibility by making sure that your daily job activities are "about" what your organization says IT is "about" ... by *standing up* for what your organization says it *stands for*. And in today's challenging business environment, doing that involves VALUES and it involves ETHICS. Both are critical to staying employed and building a successful career.

Look around your workplace. What's posted on the walls ... what's written in handbooks and guidebooks ... what's printed on brochures and newspaper inserts ... what does it say on the pins or colored vests that you may wear? Somewhere, you'll find words that describe the beliefs and business principles that your organization espouses to. And chances are, within those words is some type of promise to provide high-quality service to all customers. Who are those words written for? YOU! Who is intended to abide by those words and continually do the right thing? YOU! Who is expected to deliver the superior customer service those words are intended to guarantee? YOU! Who has the responsibility for WALKING THE TALK? Take a wild guess. It's YOU!

Values and ethics represent the core of any organization. And all you have to do is read the newspaper or watch the evening news to know that they are more important now than ever before. They are your guideposts – pointing the way to what's right and fair. They keep your business *in* business ... and *out* of trouble. And they help to attract and retain good customers to work *for* ... and great employees to work *with*.

Here's another lesson – this time from *Reality* 101: You earn the right to expect others to do things by doing those things yourself. And that lesson applies directly to business in general, and customer service in particular.

What do you expect from your organization and the companies you do business with as a customer? Do you expect people to be honest and fair? Do you expect to be treated with dignity and respect? Do you expect quality goods and services in exchange for your hard-earned money? Do you expect others to respect your time and keep their commitments? Of course! You expect all of those ... and a whole lot more. And it should be no surprise that *your* customers have the very same expectations of you!

Giving what you expect to get from others is called "integrity." Expecting what you fail to give, yourself, is called "hypocrisy." Don't be a hypocrite – our world already has more than enough of them. Instead, choose to be a role model of ethical behavior and quality customer service. We need all of those we can get.

> *To give real service you must add something which cannot be bought or measured with money, and that is sincerity and integrity.*
>
> ~ Douglas Adams ~

Do I Serve Right? A Self-Assessment

Read the statements below. Think about each one, and then respond as honestly as possible.

YES NO

| Y | N | 1. I understand, and consistently demonstrate through my behaviors, that serving customers is why my job exists.

| Y | N | 2. I make a conscious effort to put customers first. I typically focus on *their* needs, concerns, and conveniences rather than my own.

| Y | N | 3. I respect and value my customers' time. I'm usually prompt and efficient, and I do all I can to keep them from having to wait.

| Y | N | 4. I always acknowledge customers who are waiting for service and let them know I'll be with them as soon as possible.

| Y | N | 5. I always ask customers if it's okay to put them on hold, before leaving them to check on things, etc.

| Y | N | 6. If I have to tell customers that I can't do what they want, I always also state what I CAN do for them.

| Y | N | 7. Whenever I make promises or commitments to customers, I remember them ... and I always "deliver." My word is my bond.

| Y | N | 8. I make a conscious effort to emulate the best customer servers I've experienced in my life ... and to avoid the behaviors of the worst.

| Y | N | 9. I always take customer complaints seriously. I view them as important feedback tools to help me improve the quality of service I provide.

| Y | N | 10. When customers are frustrated and upset, I typically remain calm and avoid taking their words and behaviors personally.

| Y | N | 11. I make a special effort to DO things for my customers rather than just passing information along to them about what *they* need to do.

| Y | N | 12. I act as if customers are always right – even when they're not. I avoid arguing with them with the intent of proving them wrong.

| Y | N | 13. I understand that I have *internal* customers as well as external ones. And I consistently provide these "insiders" with the same high-quality service that I offer to patrons from "the outside."

| Y | N | 14. I consistently display a positive demeanor. No matter how upset or frustrated I may be with my organization, I avoid sharing my discontent with customers.

Y **N** 15. When customers are inconvenienced, I always apologize – and I give them something extra as compensation for their trouble.

Y **N** 16. I pay special attention to my "body language." I make a <u>conscious</u> effort to avoid displaying negative, distracting gestures to my customers.

Y **N** 17. I am knowledgeable of, and familiar with, ALL of the products and services my organization offers. I can describe /explain them to customers completely and accurately.

Y **N** 18. I consistently try to exceed customer expectations. After I meet their needs, I look for additional things to do for them.

Y **N** 19. I help others serve. Besides taking care of my customers, I pitch in and help my coworkers serve their customers whenever I can.

Y **N** 20. I make a <u>conscious</u> effort to avoid assumptions when serving my customers. I typically probe, ask, and listen – to make sure I understand and have met customers' needs rather than assuming I know.

Y **N** 21. I got into the customer service business – and I stay in it – because I truly enjoy helping other people.

Y **N** 22. I make a special effort to ensure that my work does not result in additional work for my customers.

Y **N** 23. I display an "attitude of gratitude." I appreciate my customers and the opportunity to serve them. And I show it through my behaviors.

Y **N** 24. I follow "The Golden Rule." I always give my customers the same high-quality service that I want for myself and the people I care about.

Y **N** 25. I make sure that I consistently serve with integrity. When it comes to our organizational values, operating principles, ethical guidelines, and service guarantees, I WALK THE TALK.

Now, go back and highlight each of the statements for which you checked the NO box (there should be some ... unless, of course, you're perfect). These are the areas you should work on in order to increase your service effectiveness and overall job success. Develop informal action plans, make a personal commitment to see them through, and get started. And for all those that you checked YES: Congratulations ... and keep doing what you're doing!

Closing Thoughts

In an era of sparsely staffed mega-discount stores, pump-it-yourself gas stations, and *can't reach a real person* business phone systems, we've become accustomed to a much different type of customer service than prior generations enjoyed and considered the norm. We've moved from "low tech/hi touch" to the polar opposite – "hi tech/low touch." And in many business arenas, it's clear that we're headed for "hi tech/NO touch."

Too often, it seems that "the bar" has been *lowered* rather than raised. Excellent customer service is quickly becoming the exception rather than the rule. More and more, we seem to expect less and less. We expect less, we accept less, we get less, and we *give* less. To borrow (and tweak) a familiar advertising slogan ...

It's not your grandfather's customer service!

Some would say that's just the way things are. I say it's a shame. The good news: It doesn't have to be that way. You have the power to change it. Actually you have an *obligation* to change it. The question is WILL YOU?

Does all this mean that quality customer service is completely a thing of the past? No, it doesn't. There still are many terrific servers out there. Maybe you're one of them. If so, the information in this book will help you be even better. If not, you're now equipped to become a member of that very special group.

Have the preceding pages covered every aspect of great customer service? Of course not! Did I provide everything there is to know about the subject areas addressed? No, again. No publication (or author) could ever accomplish that. What I have done is combine several personal experiences with a collection of tips and techniques that have been passed on to me, over the years, by the most effective service professionals I have ever experienced. I've tried to zero in on the information you need to build a reputation as one of the very best customer service employees around.

But there is a catch. As written, the strategies presented in this work are just words ... only good ideas. **You have to put them into ACTION in order for their value and benefits to be realized.**

So keep this book handy, re-read it periodically, refer to it often.
USE this material to help you achieve the workplace success you want and need. Use this material to help ensure that you ...

SERVE RIGHT.

As far as customers are concerned,
you are the company.

This is not a burden, but the core of your job.

You hold in your hands the power to keep
customers coming back – perhaps even to
make or break the company.

~ Ron Zemke and Kristin Anderson ~
Delivering Knock Your Socks Off Service

The Author

STEVE VENTURA is a recognized and respected
author, educator, book producer, and award-winning training
program designer. His work reflects over thirty years of human
resource development experience – both as a practitioner
and a business consultant. His prior books include
Start Right ... Stay Right, Five Star Teamwork;
Forget for Success, Walk Awhile In My Shoes;
What to Do When Conflict Happens; Who Are THEY, Anyway?;
Yes Lives in the Land of No; Lead Right; and ***Walk The Talk.***

The Publisher

Our goal at **WalkTheTalk.com** *is both simple and straightforward: to provide you and your organization with high-impact resources for your personal and professional success.*

Visit us at *walkthetalk.com* to learn more about our:

♦ Leadership and Employee Development Centre

♦ Inspired Living Cafe

♦ Motivational Gift Books

♦ FREE Online Newsletters

♦ Inspirational Movies

♦ 360° Feedback Processes

♦ Personal Development Kits

♦ And much more!

**Contact The WALK THE TALK Team at
1.888.822.9255
Or visit us at *www.walkthetalk.com***

WALKTHETALK.COM

Resources for Personal and Professional Success

Serve Right Resources

Whether you're a seasoned professional with years of customer service experience or someone just starting in that field, no matter if this is your ideal job or just one stop on a larger career journey, you need to be successful. You need to **SERVE RIGHT!**

Serve Right Personal Development Kit

The powerful kit contains 5 high-impact resources:

- ◆ Serve Right Book
- ◆ Serve Right Inspirational Movie
- ◆ Motivational screen saver
- ◆ Printable poster
- ◆ Personal action worksheet

All for only $29.95

Serve Right Book

1–24 copies **$12.95**

25–99 copies **$11.95**

100–499 **$10.95**

500 + please call

For a *FREE* Preview of the Serve Right Inspirational Movie, visit *WalkTheTalk.com*!

Serve Right Customer Service Learning Library!

The perfect tool to help everyone in your organization deliver "Best-In-Class" customer service! The "Serve Right" library includes these six powerful customer service books:

- ♦ *Serve Right*
- ♦ *180 Ways to Walk the Customer Service Talk*
- ♦ *Building Customer Loyalty*
- ♦ *Customer At The Crossroads*
- ♦ *Listen Up, Customer Service*
- ♦ *Monday Morning Customer Service*

All for only $59.95

To learn more about other Walk The Talk Learning Libraries, visit *WalkTheTalk.com*!

ORDER FORM

www.walkthetalk.com

✔️ **Please send me additional copies of SERVE RIGHT**

1-24 copies: $12.95 ea.   25-99 copies: $11.95 ea.   100-499 copies: $10.95 ea.   500+ copies: *Please Call*

SERVE RIGHT _____copies X $_____ = $_____

Additional Resources

Serve Right Personal Development Kit _____sets X $ 29.95 = $_____

Serve Right Customer Service _____sets X $ 59.95 = $_____
Learning Library

Product Total	$_____
*Shipping & Handling	$_____
Subtotal	$_____
Sales Tax:	

(Sales & Use Tax Collected on TX Customers Only) TX Sales Tax — 8.25% $_____

TOTAL (U.S. Dollars Only) $_____

---

*Shipping and Handling Charges

For actual shipping rates, please visit *WalkTheTalk.com*

Name_____ Title _____

Organization _____

Shipping Address _____

City_____ No P.O. Boxes _____ State_____ Zip _____

Phone _____ Fax _____

E-Mail_____

Charge Your Order: ❏ MasterCard ❏ Visa ❏ American Express

Credit Card Number_____ Exp. _____

❏ Check Enclosed (Payable to: WalkTheTalk.com)

❏ Please Invoice (Orders over $250 ONLY) P.O. # (required) _____

Prices effective January, 2009 are subject to change.

PHONE	ONLINE	MAIL
1.888.822.9255	www.walkthetalk.com	WalkTheTalk.com
or 972.899.8300	**FAX**	1100 Parker Square, Suite 250
M-F, 8:30 – 5:00 Central	**972.899.9291**	Flower Mound, TX 75028